A Christmas JOURNEY
An Advent Tradition

Activity Booklet

A Christmas Journey: An Advent Tradition Activity Booklet by Kayla Jarmon
Published by Tamarisk Tree Publishing

www.KaylaJarmon.com

The texts of this book are set in Compass Rose CPC, Fairytales Script, Wilder

Book formatting and cover design by The jCo Creative

Printed in the U.SA.

First Edition

ISBN: 978-1-948706-04-9

NOT FOR RESALE

As you journey through *A Christmas Journey Advent Booklet*,
please share on social media how God moves in your family with:

#AChristmasJourneyAdvent

Share the funny quirky things too! It's good to encourage others along the way. I look forward to following along!

Day 1

"The Journey"

In *A Christmas Journey*, we saw the most unlikely of friendships occur. What brought them together? The need of one another. Dog was helpless. Deer would not leave him in need, but Deer also needed help. Others came out because of curiosity, but more than simple curiosity carried them along their journey. On the way, they overcame obstacles and inner struggles, all while developing character and friendships.

In the Scriptures, God reveals what true friendship is. God called Abraham his friend in James 3:23. He said David was a man after his own heart in Acts 13:22. Jesus called us his friends in John 15:15. David and Jonathan and Ruth and Naomi are good examples of true friendships between people in the Scriptures. All these friendships are steeped in covenants. Friendship means to have things in common; they are woven together with common bonds. This is precisely why we're not to be friends with the world (1 John 2:15-16). We're to be in the world but not of it. We are not to look like the world. We are to look like our Lord, with whom we have things in common.

Scripture: As we go through the Christmas season on this journey, live out Proverbs 3:5-6. Go to

Song: "O Come All Ye Faithful" by John Francis Wade (Go to KaylaJarmon.com for lyrics.)

Activity: Go to KaylaJarmon.com to get the recipe for Friendship Bread. This is the most amazing bread, and your old friends and new ones will love it! It ties into our theme of friendship perfectly. You'll make your starter and knead it every day. Your kiddos will love this activity too! Today you will make your starter for your Friendship Bread.

Don't forget to share your journey with **#AChristmasJourneyAdvent**

Day 2
"Prayer"

In *A Christmas Journey*, there is much prayer. The girl's parents prayed for the puppy for Christmas, and that she would receive and love it. The Christmas Woman prayed the animals would come to her if she could help them. The other animals prayed they'd find the girl as the sleigh pulled away. The animals prayed for Dog when they found his kennel empty. And Dog prayed for Deer and his friends after he was freed from his cage.

Prayer is the vehicle that brings God into a situation. Sin interrupted our walking with God face to face, but Christ made a way for us to walk in communion with him through prayer. While we are in this fallen world we're to pray for God to intervene in our needs, wants, and situations. While Christ walked on the earth, he depended on prayer. If the son of God depended on prayer, how much more should we? In fact, our prayers are fragrant aromas before God (Revelation 5:8).

Scriptures: Revelation 5:8, 8:3-4 (Prayers of the saints.) Psalm 141:2

Song: "Breath of Heaven" by Amy Grant/Chris Eaton (Go to KaylaJarmon.com for lyrics.)

Bread: Knead the Friendship Bread Starter

Activity: As you enjoy the fragrances from these activities, I pray their fragrant aroma reminds you of how God enjoys the aroma of our prayers.

Option 1: Set out a bowl of cinnamon sticks or potpourri to enjoy the fragrance.

Option 2: On the stove, simmer two tablespoons of cinnamon. Watch the water. It evaporates! You'll do a similar simmer on Day Seven. So, look ahead and get those ingredients. This fragrance is awesome at Christmas time! My family recognizes it immediately, and it's officially the Christmas season.

Don't forget to share your journey with **#AChristmasJourneyAdvent**

Day 3

"Miracle"

John stated in his gospel (John 21:25), that if everything Christ did were written down in detail, he supposed the whole world could not contain the books that would be written. I think he's trying to get across that Christ did a ton of good works and miracles!

Miracles are discussed throughout *A Christmas Journey*. The Fire Marshall said it was a miracle the family made it out of their burning house. Mama prayed for the dog to arrive in time for Christmas. Deer said Dog needed a miracle to make it to the girl for Christmas. The miracle of Christmas, i.e., Christ being born, was discussed at the Christmas farm.

Scriptures: The miracle of Christ's birth. A virgin shall be with child. Isaiah 7:14; Matthew 1:23; Luke 1:35; Jesus directed to pray to the Lord of the harvest to send out workers into his harvest Matthew 9:37-38.

Song: "Mary Did You Know?" by Mark Lowry (Go to KaylaJarmon.com for lyrics.)

Bread: Knead Friendship Bread Starter

Activity: Gather as a family and pray about being the hands and feet of Christ during this Christmas season. Ask God to show you who to reach out to to show his love. Then move forward with God. Be faithful and leave the results to him. Make paper hearts to hang as a reminder.

Go to KaylaJarmon.com for a heart template to print out!

Decorate them as you wish. Use colored paper, glue and glitter, neon markers, you choose! Be creative. You may wish to hot glue or string embroidery floss at the top so you can hang on your Christmas tree or garland. Let them remind you to be the hands and feet of Christ to show his love to the world.

Don't forget to share your journey with **#AChristmasJourneyAdvent**

Day 4
"Fear Not"

There are more than 365 "Fear Nots" in the Bible. See https://www.soulshepherding.org/fear-not-365-days-a-year/ for details. Dr. David Jerimiah has a great study and books on that subject.

Fear is a chain that keeps us in bondage. In our story, Opossum fainted every time he was fearful. Fox was terrified and quick to believe the lies of the wolf when he was in danger. We are referred to as sheep in the Bible for good reason. Sheep follow each other around, and so do we. Have you ever been with someone who suddenly became frightened of something and started to run? Chances are high that you started to run too. You most likely thought, "What are we running from?" as you ran along with them. The other thing that sheep do is follow their master closely. So we too should follow our master, Jesus, closely. Yet there are many distractions the enemy throws at us to get us to take our eyes off of Christ. Fear is one tactic that he uses, but Christ came to break those chains of bondage from us.

After Christ died on the cross, the disciples were fearful and stayed in an upper room together. They were scared until they saw the resurrected Christ. After that, they were not fearful again. Why? They saw the ultimate end of everything: life after death. The very thing Christ had been declaring to them, they saw in action. Christ broke what sin brought to us: death's hold on us.

I work part time to help pay for things associated with my books. And yesterday, this happened at work. A little five-year-old boy walked up and said, "Excuse me." I turned to see him and said, "Yes?" He said, "Do you know Jesus?" My eyes widened, and I said, "Yes I do! Do you?" He said, "Yes, I saw that..." and pointed to a nativity and continued. "... and I wanted to ask you." I said, "Yes I do know Jesus." and stuck out my fist and we did knuckles for Christ!

A lot of people are afraid to share their faith. May I suggest that as a family you ask the Father who to share your faith with this season? It could be someone you know or a total stranger. If a stranger, you could possibly say something similar to this: "I want you to know that we celebrate Christ at Christmas, and he wants you to know that he loves you and came to earth as a baby to give his life for you, and he rose from the grave so you can live forever with him. This is the greatest gift ever."

Scriptures: John 14:27 Jesus gives us peace and tells us not to let our hearts be troubled.

Song: "It Came upon the Midnight Clear" by Edmund Sears (Go to KaylaJarmon.com for lyrics.)

Bread: Knead Friendship Bread starter

Activity: Read "A Chain of Gold" on KaylaJarmon.com.

Once you've read that, make a paper chain of garland. Cut 1" strips of paper and make your first strip into a ring and tape or glue it together. Slide your next strip through the ring and tape or glue it into a ring and continue for your desired length. You can either paint your strips gold, spread paste on them and sprinkle with gold glitter, or simply use gold construction paper. Hang in a special place to remind your family to "fear not" and live out their faith for him.

Don't forget to share your journey with **#AChristmasJourneyAdvent**

Day 5
"Calling"

Think about the bells in *A Christmas Journey*. Bells have a purpose: they're for signaling, just like on the sleigh. Church bells signal the time. Dinner bells signal to come to dinner. Door bells signal that company has arrived. Bells over shop doors signal the opening and closing of doors.

The animals in *A Christmas Journey* each had a unique purpose. Together, God used them for the greater good. Think about the members of your family. Everybody has their own role in the family. Today's activity is a way to discuss and remind us of the importance of our different roles. After the activity, discuss how they work for the common good of the family and the world.

Example Questions: What are some of Daddy's roles? What are some of Mama's roles? What are the children's roles? How do our roles correspond to others, e.g., siblings to each other, children to parents, parents to children, and Mama and Daddy to each other? How do these roles reflect God to the world and within our home?

There are specific roles in your family, and God designed it that way. He gives each of us strengths and weakness so that we need each other. And ultimately we need God to fill us so that we move in his strength and love. Begin asking God to show your family where and how he has gifted and strengthened the members of your family. Begin intentionally living your calling within your family. This will equip and prepare you to live your calling outside the walls of your home.

Scriptures: Romans 12:1-2

Song: "Go Tell it on the Mountain" by John Wesley Work, Jr. (Go to KaylaJarmon.com for lyrics.)

Bread: Knead Friendship Bread starter

Activity: Make cards with all the roles you see in your family. Then hang some bells on your door. Every time you hear them, let them remind you of your unique roles in your family and in life. God made you to shine for him in all areas and seasons of life!

Don't forget to share your journey with **#AChristmasJourneyAdvent**

Day 6

"Faith"

In *A Christmas Journey* we see the beginning of their journey kick off with a thick fog. I have an experience with extremely thick fog.

I drove through fog as thick as pea soup in the mountains one night. There were just patchy places of fog here and there in the beginning. I wondered if I should pull off the interstate. Unfamiliar with the place, I made my decision based on the patchiness of the fog and drove onward. I quickly found out that was the wrong choice. The fog thickened without warning, and there was no place (that I could see) to get off the interstate. I grasped the steering wheel, hard. The family was asleep. I was too stressed to wake my husband. Waking him would be a distraction I couldn't handle. I prayed, hard. I asked God to help me. I was terrified. I could only see the white line on the right side of the road here and there. I couldn't stop; that would cause someone to hit me. I couldn't get off and risk driving off a cliff. I had to push forward, so I prayed. I continued to pray. Did I mention that I was terrified?

Then all of a sudden, a car passed me. What?? Who in their right mind would pass someone in this fog? I couldn't believe it! Then I realized that I could see their tail lights! I would follow them! And I did. I continued to pray. I knew if that car drove off a cliff, I would follow. I had to trust they could see. After all, they passed me.

Now that was faith in action. My actions relied on the car in front of me. I would die following that car because I was not going to veer off that path. It was my only hope. Once we drove out of the fog, I wondered about the crazy person who drove past me in the thickest fog I've ever seen. Was it an answer to my prayer? Did God send that car? Was it an angel? I don't know, but I do know that it taught me a great lesson on faith.

"Faith is action based upon belief sustained by confidence."
Gene Scott

My actions followed my belief that the car in front of me could see. I would not veer from following him.

Scriptures: This Christmas remember that Adam and Eve were saved looking for the promised Messiah (Genesis 3:15). Including Abraham, Jacob, Isaac, David, etc., (Acts 8), all the Old Testament saints were saved looking for him. The disciples, Matthew, Mark, Luke, and John, were saved by faith while looking at the promised Messiah. We are saved by faith looking back to the Messiah who came as promised and died for our sins, was buried, and after three days, raised to life (1Corinthians 15). Joy to the world, the Lord has come!

Song: "Hark! The Herald Angels Sing" by Felix Mendelssohn (Go to KaylaJarmon.com for lyrics.)

Bread: Knead Friendship Bread starter

Activity: Blindfold a member of the family. Walk them to another place in the house. Turn them in three circles. Then guide them to the Christmas tree with only your directions. The person blindfolded needs to listen carefully and follow your directions to make it to the Christmas tree. This fun activity will teach a simple action of faith: they need to believe and depend on your directions and follow them.

Day 7

"Differences"

I recommend you start this day with an activity that will enhance the point. Simmer on the stove some water, cinnamon, cloves, nutmeg, and orange slices. I intentionally left these other ingredients out on Day Two's activity. I want you to appreciate the nuances each element brings to the aroma. The cinnamon and clove can be the actual whole woody spices, or it can be pre-ground. Just sprinkle a good amount in... I like considerably more cinnamon than clove... clove is very strong. Add the sliced oranges and enjoy the amazing aroma! Simmer this special mixture throughout the Christmas season. You and your family will enjoy the beautiful aroma these different elements create. Again, my family knows it's the Christmas season when I start simmering this combination. Watch the water and add some as needed; it will evaporate with the steam. Once you've started simmering this, read the story below that accompanies the day. And if you don't have oranges, it's just as lovely without them. You can simmer again once you get some!

The family of God is made of different people from different individual families. God calls and equips his children to participate in his family as a whole while seeking the common good. Think of our story. There were different animals from different families that came together. Each was equipped for the purpose of the common goal, and life events brought out those elements. Each one was needed and contributed to their journey and friendship.

When you enter into God's family, he gives gifts to his children to be used for the common good and goal. We each have different gifts, personalities, strengths, and weaknesses. We are designed that way so that we need each other. We all need each other to thrive on our journey.

Scriptures: Romans 12, 1 Corinthians 12

Song: "Do You Hear What I Hear?" by Noël Regney (Go to KaylaJarmon.com for lyrics.)

Bread: Knead Friendship Bread starter

Activity: The gifts are found in Romans 12 and 1 Corinthians 12. Try to identify the gifts within your family. If it's something you feel passionate about, you're most likely gifted with that gift. For example, if you feel the urge to serve others frequently and notice when others are doing the same, you most likely have the gift of service. If you're passionate about people growing in their knowledge and wisdom of the Lord, you most likely have the gift of teaching.

Go to KaylaJarmon.com to see a list of all the gifts and examples of how they can be portrayed.

Don't forget to share your journey with **#AChristmasJourneyAdvent**

Day 8
"Greed"

Christ came to give life. He was born to give the best gift of all, eternal life! He literally died in our place. He stood in our place for our sin and took our punishment. He died to give us eternal life.

The enemy comes to steal, kill, and destroy. That was his goal in the Garden of Eden: he tricked Adam and Eve into death.

The wolves in A Christmas Journey portray the enemy. The wolves wanted to destroy each animal in our story. The animals came together to protect the one who couldn't protect himself, Dog. The wolves were only slowed down with each distraction the animals gave. They continued the pursuit with the entrance of another animal to chase for the kill. Finally, they met with the ultimate catch of the day, the fox. They were so greedy for gain, they would do anything to catch a fox. This climaxed with the ultimate threat from the skunk and his stink bomb of the year. The stink bomb drove the wolves away. The animals pulled together for the common good and were victorious!

Scripture: Genesis 3

Songs: You have two songs with this activity, one on greed and the other on giving. (Go to KaylaJarmon.com for lyrics.)

GREED: "I Want a Hippopotamus for Christmas" by John Rox
GIVING: "Little Drummer Boy" by Katherine Kennicott Davis

Bread: Knead Friendship Bread starter

Activity: This Christmas season, look at how you react to people and situations. Are you like the wolves and taking for yourself, or are you like Christ and thinking of the best for others? Look for ways to give to people instead of taking.

Examples:
Instead of taking the last piece of candy, or cake, or cookie, leave it for someone else. Perhaps leave a note without your name, explaining that you saw it and wanted it but decided to be like Christ and left it for the next person who wants it. BUT the next person, who comes for the treat and finds the note, must eat it and be thankful for the gift from that person.

Let someone else choose the fun activity.

Let someone else go first.

Let someone else win.

Let someone else choose the snack.

Let someone else choose what to watch.

Let someone else choose the book to read.

Do extra chores to bless Mom and Dad.

Help a sister or brother with their chores

Give the gift of thinking of others throughout this Christmas season.

Don't forget to share your journey with
#AChristmasJourneyAdvent

Day 9
"Lies"

A wolf in *A Christmas Journey* confronted the skunk by telling others not to fear the threat of the skunk. He knew the skunk's history of not wanting to spray his stink. However, he was unaware that friendship changed Skunk. Skunk learned valuable lessons of friendship, and he gave his word that if needed, he would indeed spray. He was prepared to spray his stink, and in fact, he did. This was the last surprise for the wolves, and it worked: it drove them all away.

The wolf knew only part of the truth about the skunk, and when he spoke, he spoke partial truths. That is precisely how the enemy works. He looks for the weak areas of people with which to take them down. He throws half-truths in the person's face and in the face of others to cause all kinds of bad emotions such as fear, anger, division, etc.

As Fox listened to the partial truths of the wolf, he began believing him and doubted Skunk's word. He became afraid his words would cause the skunk to turn back, but Skunk stayed true to his word. Afterwards, Skunk confronted Fox about doubting his word of friendship, and Fox learned a valuable lesson. Lies always tempt people to believe them, whether you're the one telling them or the one hearing them. Lies are not from God; they are from the evil one, who is the father of all lies.

As children of God, we are to be people of the truth because God is truth. It's important to remain in the truth. Be a person of truth. Let your yes mean yes and your no mean no (Matthew 5:37). Be like Christ. Let people around you count on your honesty to be a pillar in your life. You will point people to God as you live that way. Skunk and

Fox both grew stronger in their friendship as they realized the importance of true words.

Scriptures: Proverbs 12:22; Philippians 4:8

Song: "You're A Mean One, Mr. Grinch" by Dr. Seuss/Albert Hague (Go to KaylaJarmon.com for lyrics.)

Bread: Knead Friendship Bread starter

Activity: Cookie Fun! Go to KaylaJarmon.com for a sugar cookie recipe.

Discuss lies, what they do, and how they are presented... what harm they cause to the one speaking them, those hearing them, and those of whom the lies are spoken. You can choose from two activities. For a more frugal activity. choose the second option. Either one will be fun and drive the point home.

> **Option 1**: Make sugar cookies; one good batch with the true ingredients and one bad batch with salt in place of sugar. Place them alongside each other so you can't tell them apart. Set them out for the ultimate test.
>
> **Option 2**:Make sugar cookies with true ingredients. Sprinkle salt instead of sugar on the top of half of them before baking. Sprinkle a lot so it looks like sugar. Sprinkle sugar on the top of the other half. Place them alongside each other so you can't tell them apart. Set them out for the ultimate test.

Could you tell the difference between the true sugar cookies and the false ones? Could you tell the difference by looking at them, by how they smelled, or how they tasted? Set them out for friends to enjoy and share the importance of knowing what lies do and where they come from. This is a good example of lies and how they're packaged.

Day 10

"Truth"

In *A Christmas Journey*, there were a few lies swirling around that our friends had to overcome.

Fox had the reputation of being very prideful and arrogant simply because he was wise.

Raccoon had the reputation of being a bandit and sneaky, simply because of the coloring on his face, which looks like the mask a thief wears. In addition, they're good at picking locks and opening things.

Opossum had the reputation of faking his death. One never knew if he was truly dead or not.

Skunk had the reputation of refusing to stink. Would he really spray when needed? He did. But his reputation, what he was known for, caused others to doubt.

When Christ battled the enemy, he always spoke the truth of God to him, i.e., what the Scriptures say. God is truth. Christ is the way and the truth and the life (John 14:6). He came to give back what the enemy took away with his lies in the Garden of Eden, i.e., the way back to God.

We must take care to speak and live the truth. In the end it will always triumph. It matters not what others think of us, as long as we are walking in God's truth.

Scripture: Matthew 7

Song: "The First Noel" (Noel means birth.) by Davies Gilbert (Go to KaylaJarmon.com for lyrics.)

Bread: Knead Friendship Bread starter

Activity: Play the telephone game. This will demonstrate how easily something can get distorted. Write a phrase down that has difficult words in it. Then put it in your pocket. Take a family member in another room and whisper that phrase clearly and only once to that person. Then they do the same to the next member until it goes through the entire family. Once it reaches the last person, that person speaks the phrase out loud. Did the phrase become distorted? Discuss how God's word is the truth and how he watched over it.

Also, a great video to watch is *The Indestructable Book: The Story of the Bible*:
https://www.youtube.com/watch?v=W1ZxGhNfLew

Don't forget to share your journey with **#AChristmasJourneyAdvent**

Day 11
"Pride"

In *A Christmas Journey*, the wolves were sure of themselves as they laughed at the skunk. When Skunk did a handstand they laughed all the more. They were sure he wouldn't spray. The Scriptures tell us that pride goes before the fall. And oh how the wolves fell with Skunk's stink bomb! They fell all over themselves as they raced away from Skunk!

Watch out for pride. It shows up in all forms:

> Bullying is a form of pride.
> Lying stems from pride.
> Sarcasm is a form of pride
> Criticizing is a form of pride

Scriptures: Proverbs 16:18 (Pride goes before the fall.)
Philippians 2:5-11 (Christ emptied himself.)

As a family, we try to help each other stay far away from pride. I'll give you one funny example that my son called me on a while back. I had to run a late errand that didn't require my getting out of the car. I had my pjs on and some slip-on shoes and took my son along with me. I needed something from the store, so I stopped there and asked him to go in for me. We were having fun in the car together, so he asked me to go in with him. I told him I couldn't because I was wearing my pjs. He told me they didn't look like pjs—I was the only one who knew they were pjs. This was true. They were bigger comfy pants and a bigger long-sleeve pull-over shirt.

However, I was without make-up as well and told him this.

He called me on it and asked me if it was a form of pride in my life. I was busted. I mean, what could I say? How could I defend myself? Lie? I could stand on the pajama thing, but you couldn't tell they were pajamas, and I knew this. And no, I wasn't going to lie, but this was an option the enemy offered up to me. My son would've seen through that and would've known I lied. I had no defense. It was a form of pride. I had to overcome it. So I told him it was and that I didn't want to go in because of it. I told him it's important to overcome pride in the small areas so we can overcome in the bigger ones. So in I went to show my son how to combat pride. It was a lesson for us both, and we continued having fun together!

Song: "Away in A Manger" by William J. Kirkpatrick (Go to KaylaJarmon.com for lyrics.)

Bread: Knead Friendship Bread starter

Activity: Get a large bowl or plastic tub. Fill it with warm soapy water. Wash one another's feet. Pray for the person, aloud, while you're washing their feet. Christ did this for his disciples... we ought to for one another and share in that experience.

Don't forget to share your journey with **#AChristmasJourneyAdvent**

Day 12
"Scars"

In *A Christmas Journey*, Fox slumps in sadness as he listens to Raccoon's words about him. He tells Raccoon that others seem to always misunderstand his words. He shares how their perception of him has wounded him. He confides how he has few friends because of it.

Deer saves the day by explaining the differences in the animals and their ways. He goes on to say that they're all needed and to fight about them hinders the way. He agrees with the perception of the fox that God brought them together for the greater cause.

Just like the fox, we've all been wounded by others, and sometimes we ourselves wound others. We should ask forgiveness when we hurt others. Sometimes our hurts leave emotional scars, as some things are too hard to forget. We may remember things, but we should always forgive, since we ourselves have been forgiven so much by God.

Christ felt the hurts and pains we feel and has the scars to prove it. When he was on the cross, he asked the Father to forgive the ones that put him there, saying, "Forgive them, they know not what they do" (Luke 23:34). He prayed for those who hung him on the cross, those who spit on him, and those who mocked him. He forgave them.

If Christ asked God to forgive those who put him on the cross, how much more should we ask forgiveness from God and others that we-ourselves hurt? Whether we hurt with our words, deeds, or actions, we should make it right, and the first step is to ask for forgiveness.

Scriptures: 1 Peter 2:20-25

Song: "Joy to the World" by George Frideric Handel (Go to KaylaJarmon.com for lyrics.)

Bread: Knead Friendship Bread starter

Activity: Firefighters work to save others from being consumed in fires. Fires leave horrible scars. When we hurt others, it can leave scars that we can't see. It leaves scars on their hearts and minds. To help us remember that our wrongs cause scars, take some cookies/goodies to those who snatch others from scar-causing flames. Take them to your local fire department with a Christmas card and/or a special note. And pray God will remind you of the scars our wounding others can make.

Don't forget to share your journey with **#AChristmasJourneyAdvent**

Day 13
"Forgiveness"

In *A Christmas Journey*, When Raccoon asked for forgiveness, Fox slapped his hand away but gave him a big bear hug instead. Fox was quick to forgive. We too should be quick to forgive.

God says in Matthew 18:21-35 that we must forgive others from the heart, or we too will be in bondage. Unforgiveness makes us a prisoner in our own hearts and lives. It keeps us in bondage to bitterness that grows with the passing of time. And a root of bitterness defiles the many (Hebrews 12:15). It does not stay with you alone. If we forgive from the heart, we are free.

This is tricky. I learned this lesson in life. I went through the Christian formalities of forgiving someone for something. I did as God's word tells us to and forgave the person. We talked of Scripture and handled it all as the Scriptures guide us to.

A few weeks later, I was at church, and my whole family was present as a niece was getting baptized. They opened the altar for anyone who wanted to go down to pray before the Lord. I began praying that a lost brother of mine would go down there. As I was praying, I felt the Lord tell me I needed to go down there. I thought, "Me? No it's my brother who needs it. Why would I need it?" I recognized the following dialogue as truth. God said, "You haven't forgiven ________. "I argued, "Yes I have." Then he said, "From the heart." I immediately knew this to be truth! I had walked through all the formalities of forgiveness, yet I had not forgiven from the heart. I recognized immediately that I had erected walls in my heart towards this person. I went forward, a repentant, broken person.

How could I have done that? I knew pride was at the center of it. I verbally forgave, but I was irritated that I had to go through it at all. I was broken and asked the Lord to forgive me. Who was I to harbor anything in my heart when God had forgiven me so much? As soon as I did forgive, my erected walls crumbled, and I was free, and I felt this freedom. I had been a prisoner to bitterness, unbeknownst to me, and the freedom of true forgiveness blasted it away. I told God I would share with that person and ask for their forgiveness too. I did, and we healed from it God's way.

This experience was Matthew 18:21-35 lived out. Christ came in forgiveness and mercy. He opened the way to God for us. He came to show us how to live in this fallen world, God's way.

Scriptures: Matthew 18:21-35; Hebrews 12:15.

Song: "God Rest Ye Merry Gentlemen" by George Frideric Handel (Go to KaylaJarmon.com for lyrics.)

Bread: Knead Friendship Bread starter

Activity: Ask forgiveness for something you recently did or for a way that you acted. Ask God to show you if there is any unforgiveness in your heart.

Make angel wings to represent freedom. Be creative on your own, or you can go to KaylaJarmon.com for a pattern to print. Date the backside and write your name on it. Cut them out, spread glue or paste on them, and sprinkle glitter on them. When they dry, put some glue or hot glue on the back with a loop of embroidery floss. When dry, hang on your tree as a reminder of the freedom that forgiveness brings.

Don't forget to share your journey with **#AChristmasJourneyAdvent**

Day 14
"Friendship"

In *A Christmas Story*, our friends did not start out as friends but ended as the greatest of friends. Friends have things in common. They are intertwined with common interests, and we saw this grow with our friends in the story. They had no common interests with the wolves.

We're told in the Scriptures that we are to be in the world but not of it. And if you're a friend with the world you are hostile with God (James 4:4). This is because friendships bind you together. You have common interests that are intertwined in your friendships. This is why we're warned to choose our friends carefully. Bad company corrupts good morals (1Corinthians 15:33). This is also why we're to marry other believers. If the person one marries isn't a child of God he/she will lead the other astray.

The most beautiful marriages I've seen are those who love God and have continued growing in the Lord together. Oh how strong and beautiful their marriages are!

Scripture: John 15:13; Greater love has no one than to lay his life down for his friends; James 3:23 Abraham believed God, and he was called a friend of God; John 15:15 Christ calls us friends; James 4:4 If you wish to be a friend of the world, you make yourself an enemy of God.

Song: "We Three Kings of Orient Are" by John Henry Hopkins Jr. (Go to KaylaJarmon.com for lyrics.)

Bread: Knead Friendship Bread starter

Activity: Write notes with at least three things you love about each of your family members. You can write as much as you want but write at least three things. You'll put these notes in their stockings, and on Christmas Eve you'll read them aloud. You have 10 days to complete this activity and get them in their stockings. Begin today and if need be, continue it over the next few days. Pray and ask God to show you things. Don't put it off! Write something every day. If the Lord shows you something new about someone, add to what you've already written about them.

Don't forget to share your journey with
#AChristmasJourneyAdvent

Day 15
"God's Sovereignty"

In *A Christmas Journey*, God worked through everything, and once we've read the story through, it's easy to see! That's how it is in life too. When we get to the other side of things, we can see how God worked in all things. We won't know some things until we see him face to face. Then we will know and see how he worked in everything. For now, we live in this three-dimensional world where time is linear. We can only see the present and the past. That's why after reading A Christmas Journey you can see how God worked in all things. It's now in the past, but as you read it, it was unfolding to you as you read.

God is outside of our three-dimensional world. He is outside of time. He sees the end from the beginning. This is precisely why his prophecies could be foretold, and why they came true and will come true.

Scriptures: Read through these passages on God's sovereignty. These Scriptures are after Joseph was sold into slavery by his brothers. This was the outcome and Joseph could see God's sovereignty: Genesis 42:6; 45:5, 7-8; 50:20.

In Matthew 1 we see the coming of Messiah as promised. The book of John mentions the appointed time several times and reveals God's plan in motion. God knows the end from the beginning.

Song: "O come, O come, Emmanuel" by Thomas Helmore
Go to KaylaJarmon.com for lyrics.

Bread: Knead Friendship Bread starter

Activity: Make a shoebox Christmas village. Cut out a square in the front of the box. Decorate the inside of the box. As a family, make little houses out of Legos, popsicle sticks, toothpicks, etc. Use your imagination. Place them in your village where you want them. Look through the window to see how they look where you placed them. Once they're where you want them, paste or hot-glue them down if you wish. Hot-glue is faster but it's hot, so be careful!

Next, paste or glue down some snow. Cotton makes great snow. Add little trees and plants to make a winter wonderland. You can buy little trees or cut some tiny branches from your evergreens, etc. to glue down. Add little cars for the roads. Use your imagination!

Once you're finished with your house, look through the window at your three-dimensional world. When you look through the window, you can see the front side of your town. However, when you observe the village from the top of the box, you can see the entire town all at once. Imagine a car driving through your town. From above, you would be able to see the end from the beginning as it drives throughout the town.

God is outside of time: he sees the end from the beginning. This is but one of the attributes of his sovereignty.

Extra fun: Once you've observed this, place a piece of white tissue on the top of the box. You can tape the sides down. This gives a cool-toned-white-light effect to your town... kind of resembles a cloud-covered snowy day.

Don't forget to share your journey with **#AChristmasJourneyAdvent**

Day 16

"Purpose"

In *A Christmas Journey*, we saw the unique purpose of each character toward the common goal. The common goal was to get Dog to the girl in time for Christmas. The dog was going to become part of a family, and every character along the way became a life-long friend and family member through their journey.

God loves family. God wanted a family. God initiated family. God made man and said it's not good for man to be alone. He made Eve for Adam and said, "Be fruitful and multiply and fill the earth." God wanted a family.

God put you on earth through your birth into a family. Then when you become God's child, you're born again into his family. As his children, we are to glorify God and point people to him. Christ came into this world by being born of a virgin, i.e., a supernatural birth. We celebrate that at Christmas. Christ was born, and he grew, lived, and died while showing people how to live on this earth while walking with God. God made us to be lights in this dark world, and we're to shine brightly for him!

Scriptures: Matthew 5:14-16 (A city on a hill can't be hidden.)

Song: "I Heard the Bells on Christmas Day" by Henry Wadsworth Longfellow/John Calkin
(Go to KaylaJarmon.com for lyrics.)

Bread: Knead Friendship Bread starter

Activity: Put lights up in a special window as a reminder.

Just like the lights are all connected in one strand, so are we within our family. And together we shine brightly for him!

Day 17
"Kindness"

In *A Christmas Journey*, we see the kindness and goodness of God. The car transporting Dog could have made it to town in time had there been no fog. But the fog caused Dog to meet Deer, Skunk, Fox, Opossum, Raccoon, and the Christmas Woman. It caused the animals and Dog to learn of the true meaning of Christmas. It caused them to come together as friends and family. It caused them to overcome internal and external obstacles together. It caused them to know God and the reason for our being here. Although our story is fictional, things like this happen all the time. God is good, and we see his goodness and kindness all around us.

Scriptures: Matthew 5:45; Titus 3:3-5; Romans 2:4 (Kindness of God leads to repentance.)

Song: "Silent Night" by Franz Xaver Gruber/Joseph Mohr (Go to KaylaJarmon.com for lyrics.)

Bread: Knead Friendship Bread starter (keep going!)

Activity: Be kind to others, showing them the true meaning of Christmas. Leave a special note and goodies for your mail person or those who pick up the garbage on your street. Offer to help a neighbor or surprise a family on your street with goodies. Make someone's bed. Do something special for someone.

Don't forget to share your journey with **#AChristmasJourneyAdvent**

Day 18
"Inward Witness"

In *A Christmas Journey*, Dog began to see how God was answering prayers and how he was leading all things to work together for good. He sensed that the animals at the Christmas Woman's house knew something about the baby in the manger, and he sensed it was true and wanted it too. When he finally found the town and was weary, he was excited to find the manger scene. He went and lay next to the baby Jesus. He felt and knew the truth of God and its peace. The Scriptures for today speak well to what is known by all.

Scriptures: James 1:21; Romans 1:15-25 (Engrafted Word, internal witness.)

Song: "What Child Is This" by William Chatterton Dix (Go to KaylaJarmon.com for lyrics.)

Bread: Knead Friendship Bread starter

Activity: Draw names in the family. Share something true and sweet about that person. (You can also have each person share something true and sweet about every member.) After everyone has shared, ask each person:

How did you feel when that was shared about you?

Because that was true, you identified and resonated with it. Now examine how that made you feel inside. This is an inward witness. In a similar way, we sense that same thing about the truth of God, even before we are his child. He made us that way, and he created the world in such a way that creation speaks for him too.

This is a great activity for today's discussion, but it is a wonderful addition to do regularly! Our family has gotten together following church services and spoken these words of affirmation to each other and we are all so blessed to hear them! However often this is done, it is such a great blessing!

Day 19
"Strengths"

In *A Christmas Journey*, each animal had a unique strength that was needed for the journey. They had to grow in their weak areas. Together they helped one another grow, but oh how they shone in their strengths and how God made them!

Deer could carry the dog on his antlers. Opossum had opposable thumbs with which to pull the cage off Deer's antlers. Skunk had the stinker that saved the day. Fox could plan and orchestrate things. Raccoon was a great helper and htinker. He was used to help fox grow in many ways. They all needed each other!

We need each other too. Instead of complaining about weaknesses of others, help them shine and grow stronger. Let's recognize, exhort, and encourage one another to great things together!!!

Scriptures: Let's consider the design of the Gospels and how each has a unique purpose woven within:
Matthew presents Jesus Christ as the Messiah, the Lion of the tribe of Judah. Mark presents Jesus Christ in his role as the suffering servant. Luke, being a doctor, emphasizes Jesus Christ as the Son of Man. John presents Jesus Christ as the Son of God.

https://www.youtube.com/watch?v=i9wAIjxBZtY

Song: "O Little Town of Bethlehem" by Phillips Brooks (Go to KaylaJarmon.com for lyrics.)

Bread: Knead Friendship Bread starter

Activity: Do what you do best! Discuss the possibilities of a family project where each person's strength shines. No matter how big or small the project, find an area to glorify God with how he made you. Ask God for his wisdom to see the strengths he gave to the individuals in your family.

Don't forget to share your journey with **#AChristmasJourneyAdvent**

Day 20

"Greater Cause"

In *A Christmas Journey*, we see the greater cause was to get Dog to the girl in time for Christmas. There were many details that came together to get him to her. There were also many obstacles they had to overcome. Whether the enemy caused the obstacles or not didn't matter. Prayers were lifted, and they came together. In the end, everyone felt God's love over, in, and through it all. In the sovereignty of God each thing, person, and animal aligned with the common goal and good. In the end, everyone felt God's love over, in, and through it all.

As we go along life's journey, we should remember to keep the greater cause in mind. We should seek God's heart in all things. He's always working!

Scriptures: Timothy learned faith from his grandmother: 2 Timothy 1:5-6; Priscilla and Aquila explained the way of God more accurately to Apollos: Acts 18:24-26. Ruth and Naomi's relationship: the book of Ruth.

Song: "Mary's Little Boy Child" by Jester Hairston
(Go to KaylaJarmon.com for lyrics.)

Bread: Knead Friendship Bread starter

Activity: Identify the greater cause in life:
Why were we put here by God? We know we are to glorify God and point people to him. That's our greater cause in life.

Now discuss how this greater cause can be applied to your own family.
What is the greater cause in your family?
Do you have a greater cause?

Should you have a greater cause?
Do you have a common goal for the good of others?
What is the greater cause for the parents in your family?
What is the greater cause for the children in your family?

By having this conversation, it unifies the family and gives a good common goal and cause. Consider making a mission statement for your family. It's an excellent way to keep forging on towards that greater cause you've identified!

Day 21

"Thanksgiving"

In *A Christmas Journey*, the animals traveled a long way. They went through trials and overcame them. When they arrived at the Christmas Woman's place, they witnessed God answering many prayers. She herself had been praying for them and asked God to lead them to her if she could help them. And he did. She knew God could send them to her, so she readied herself, as well as her team of horses.

Once our friends were in the sleigh, with their own special treats, they were moved to thanksgiving with how God brought everything together.

Scriptures: Philippians 4:6-7

Song: "Angels We Have Heard on High" by James Chadwick (Go to KaylaJarmon.com for lyrics.)

Activity: Write cards of thanksgiving to God for what he has done for you and/or your family. Decorate a box of your choice—a wooden one, a shoe box—any type. Decorate it beautifully and place the cards inside. Place the box under the tree. Read your cards together, and every Christmas pull the cards out and reflect on your thanksgivings! Add new ones each year.

This is an awesome way to stir up thanksgiving within your family. For a special treat, listen to "The Weapons of Our Warfare: Rejoicing" by Otto Koning. You can find it online.

Don't forget to share your journey with **#AChristmasJourneyAdvent**

Day 22
"Love"

In *A Christmas Journey*, the girl lost her dog in a house fire. God moved her parents to purchase a new puppy for her. He moved people to pray for her and her new puppy. He moved the animals to join together to help get Dog get to her. He moved the Christmas Woman to pray, asking God to bring them to her if she could help them. He even used the wolves to chase them closer to the Christmas Woman's place. He brought the snow, which made her lights noticeable from a distance. He led Dog to town, and his friends too. He did all of this while drawing them closer to him and to each other. He gave the girl a dream revealing Dog to her, and she recognized him. Christmas Woman filled in all the details for the parents. Everyone saw God's hand of love in and through it all.

Stories like this happen all over the world, and none of these stories could take place if God had not intervened and given us his son to make a way back to him. Without Christ, we would stand guilty and condemned before God, but God in his love provided a way through Christ, the babe born in a manger.

Scriptures: John 3:16

Song: "The Face of Love" by Jewel Kilcher
Go to KaylaJarmon.com for lyrics and a site to watch/hear the song. I love this song! It's one of my favorite Christmas songs. It's a beautiful picture of understanding, receiving, and loving Christ.

Activity: It's time! Follow the directions on the Friendship Bread and bake! Take some Friendship Bread along with some of the starter to special friends. Use it as an opportunity to teach about friendship and loving others well.

You can also take cookies and leave them at the door for someone who acts distant to you, or to someone less fortunate. Showing love to others no matter what.

Day 23
"Christ"

In *A Christmas Journey*, we were reminded of the reason for the season: Christ.

- as the animals came together for the good of another.
- as the animals listened to Deer explain the miracle of Christmas.
- as they learned about the Christmas miracle that takes place on Christmas Woman's farm.
- as the animals sensed something special about the babe in the manger scene.
- by the prayers being lifted up.
- by the emphasis on love and family.
- by seeing God's heart for his family.

We celebrate Christ during Christmas. He is the reason for the season. I pray that *A Christmas Journey* has moved you closer to God and caused you to reflect on him more this Christmas. Praying you continue to reflect him brightly!

Scriptures: Luke 2:1-12

Song: "Sweet Little Jesus Boy" by Robert MacGimsey (Go to KaylaJarmon.com for lyrics.)

Activity: Make cards that say, Jesus is the reason for the season! Leave them for people to find.

Don't forget to share your journey with **#AChristmasJourneyAdvent**

Day 24

"Family and Greater Cause"

Everyone in *A Christmas Journey* realized that the love everyone felt was coming down from above. They knew God brought them together in answer to prayer. They felt something special was happening in their individual lives and in the lives of those connected to the town.

With Christ in your heart, you instinctively move in love to those around you. Our friends instinctively anticipate this for the town they now call home.

I hope *A Christmas Journey* has carried you to the throne of God this Christmas. Celebrate the Christ child born in a manger!

Scripture: Isaiah 7:14; John 15 (Abide in him!)

Song: "O Holy Night" by Adolphe Adam/Placide Cappeau (Go to KaylaJarmon.com for lyrics.)

Activity: Read the notes in your stockings. Read them aloud so others are encouraged. Give thanksgiving to God for all he has done.

Have a wonderful Christmas with your family!
Merry Christmas! Praise his holy name!

Notes and Memories

35296098R00030

Made in the USA
Columbia, SC
20 November 2018